This City

The
Kathleen Grattan
Award for Poetry
2010

JENNIFER COMPTON
This City

OTAGO

Published by Otago University Press
Level 1/398 Cumberland Street
PO Box 56
Dunedin
New Zealand
Email: university.press@otago.ac.nz
Fax: 64 3 479 8385

First published 2011
Copyright © Jennifer Compton 2011
ISBN 978 1 877578 10 6

With thanks to the Kathleen Grattan Estate and Trustees

Publisher: Wendy Harrex
Designer: Fiona Moffat
Cover photograph: Isabella Harrex
Printed in Hong Kong through Condor Production Ltd.

Contents

In Australia

This City

I am travelling away from my life, towards my life.

This city knows all my secrets.

And that tram, lit from within, waiting at the end of the line.

This city, which is nowhere else.

In Italy

Approaching Firenze

A manifestation on a piece of waste land, a thousand men
in uniform, all of them young. Some of them will die soon.

In the scheme of things some of them are dead, have died.
We all die. Some are old men. Living in Mondsee or Ulm.

But in this moment, lifted out of what is called time, they are
young. The stink of success and their prowess evaporates,

diffuses like a mist, a heady, foxy, delicious, momentary thing.
They stand easy, the whisper of the cloth that folds them sings.

Soon they will eat. Soon they will sleep. They took the city, now
they can lose the city, and they will. But they spare the old bridge.

Open City

Like breathing out forever, we announce our imminent absence.
The oracle told each of us at the same time in a specific voice
that the great conversation of armed rhetoric and counter-attack,

that the flags and insignia, the fine, high step, the articulate whelp
we groomed as a mascot, the port of the mess, the broadside, dog
help us, the grunt and the mud and that lost night when we slept

were ridiculous. Would haunt us. That was the last night we would
sleep. Like anyone else in this city we look to the snow on the hills.
And consider our options. Or rather, what we must do. Our retreat.

Another Language

My ancient husband and I
are strolling Rapallo
like locals because
of the locals we know.

Taking the air
promenading
in this town
lived Ezra Pound.

Another ancient couple
approaches us.
He seizes her elbow
hisses in her face –

Stupida Italiana!
I flinch. Vicious.
I heard it as
– unmediated –

You stupid Italian woman!
Something in my brain
knew what he said.
And she flinched, too.

On The Waterfront In Genoa, Just Before Dawn, At Chucking Out Time

I asked the kids from Piazza delle Erbe who had led me here what the club was called because it had no sign. *Si chiama Pussycats* – they said.

It was two rooms in a warehouse up a flight of stairs. The music was loud. They had run out of white wine.

The kids took off and I sat myself down on a step made of stone. I didn't know where I was and had to figure out how to get home.

A young man, made of ebony, from Senegal or Somalia or the Côte d'Ivoire, sat down beside me gracefully.

Here you might think – Well well. But it wasn't like that. He sat next to me as if I was his mother, or his grandmother. I'm old. He was young.

I told him where I was from. He bent his head. Australia. Oh fortunate one. When I asked him about his country he leapt to his feet and sang.

Oh Mama ... Mama Africa. Oh Mama ... Mama Africa. He danced and sang. Then the tears came. A boy the age of my son.

I had a chocolate in my purse and I gave it to him. I don't think I know what hungry is. A stuttering and blind urgent cramming thing.

And yes, but don't tell anyone, I gave him the twenty euro that I had to hand. Stammering, ill at ease, he asked me what I had in mind.

It disgraced us both that he had to ask what the traffic between us was. But we strolled on. I bought him a stand up coffee at an early bar.

I had to order it because the girl wouldn't serve him. Her look of disdain. And then I said – *Goodbye, my friend.* And I went home.

The House Of Wives

1.

Ah – he said. Camogli. Casa delle mogli. The house of wives.
Because their husbands were fishermen and so always at sea.

Or it can mean houses packed close together. The village
like one house with many wives, calling out to each other

from their windows. Or, further back, after the deity, Camuli.
A sound too much like Ca'mogli to let the happy joke go past

But – I replied. If they were fishermen then many would
have been drowned dead. The house of widows instead.

That is not the Italian way. We infer, we imply, we don't say.
But now, of course, it is for the tourists, they sell ice cream.

2.

Paddling on the pebble beach – ouch ouch – I come upon
a blue clothes peg, her function intact, at the high tide line.

Back in Australia my pegs had gone missing mysteriously
then one day we found a satin bowerbird's courtship avenue.

The males adore blue, filch drinking straws and bottle tops
and pegs. What had been vanishing was always and only blue.

They used to make do with berries and flowers, which faded,
but amcoplast solvent drives them on to a fresh excess of art,

brandishing the fetish, strutting and tossing, laying it down pat.
This very peg flies home, a gift from Camogli to our bowerbirds.

In New Zealand

Musical Buildings

You have been playing musical buildings while I
have been away, visiting the world. And you have

been laying landmines, subtle, fragrant explosions
hoisting me, as I walk your streets, into an original

thought – it is a cunning city. Not what it was, yet
nothing is forgotten. As a tree dies, another grows.

My library in Lyall Bay is given over to private use
but the magic door up to the free books is still there.

The Bank of New Zealand, opposite James Smiths,
is now a Burger King. James Smiths has absconded.

Wellington Central Library is the City Gallery, ok?
It's the Botanic Garden, not the Botanical Gardens.

It never has been the Botanical Gardens. That's just
what the locals like to call it in their whimsical way.

The National Art Gallery and Dominion Museum
are part of the Massey campus, I would swear they

had kept the linoleum if it wasn't so patently new.
It squeaks underfoot with an eerie Proustian effect.

Wellington District Ambulance is now a wine bar.
The Public Trust houses Creative New Zealand.

Athletic Park has gone. So have the dangerous
playgrounds with their battering rams with which

we tried to kill each other and, mostly, didn't succeed.
There was always one kid who would throw up though

if you kept on pushing higher while he screamed – *Stop!*
And there is the building still decked out as E. Morris Jnr

where I viewed my father's bedizened body in his coffin,
which now trades in coffee and cake as Strawberry Fare.

Moxham Ave

I folded my book shut primly
glanced out of the bus window
there were the big boys cycling
to school like the big boys do.

His front wheel caught in gravel
and as he fell he caught my eye
I am the last person he saw as he
fell gracefully under the wheels.

In his eyes, wild surmise – *Is this ...?*
He said – *I'm falling. Will I die?*
I said – *Yes.* As I reached to save him.
And then I couldn't see him any more.

That was one godawful, unholy crunch.
A woman stood up in the bus, screamed
– *That was his bike! That was his bike!*
But I don't think any of us believed her.

John Mardell ran like a wild person
up and down all the long front paths
hammering on the doors, not waiting
long enough for anyone to answer.

Much too late. We had ridden that crunch.
The driver froze in an irretrievable moment
– his foot stamped on the brake – then leapt
in an impossible arc out of his seat and into

what came next.

The Pines

I remember you driving the corniche past The Pines from Island Bay to Lyall Bay.
I was visiting from Australia, you had invited me to a party, it was dull. In spite of
the people toking in an upstairs room. I stood to dance and you hissed – *Sit down!*
The tattooed men who were arriving took a woman dancing on her own as an open
invitation. I sat down and whined that I wanted to go home.

As you ground the gears I became aware you had been upstairs and the green was
messing with your mind. The car was rocketing, lurching, hurtling. I glanced down
at Breaker Bay and in the extremity of my fear spoke as your older sister – *I know
you THINK!!! you are driving slowly but you are actually driving very very fast.*
You rolled a disbelieving eye, but slowed, above the cliff.

The party got out of hand and men were fighting in the street, swinging bike chains.
The Armed Offenders Squad took up positions in yards on the hills above, locked it
down. But we had got home with a final lurch and left the car parked askew, ajangle.
But that is all by the by, it had been in my mind. As if it was my only memory of you.
Today you fly in from Australia for a funeral at The Pines.

The son of your best friend was driving around in cars and came to grief as so many
of the young boy racers do. Our father and our mother would go to the cabaret there,
there at The Pines. The men secreted liquor in the women's beaded evening bags or
under their fur wraps. I remember one of the outfits our mother put together. A long
black pleated skirt and a 'broidered weskit in red and gold.

I think of you at the funeral at The Pines, a mother now, someone who has survived.
I would have gone with you, it would have been fitting, and apt, but through a friend
of a friend a private viewing of local artworks had been set up at almost the same time.
And I chose that. Because those local artworks are what have always saved me. From
the dying fall.

Crunch

Syringes are not scattered
on doorsteps or in gutters
the disaffected in this city
are on methamphetamine.

Or p – which is the pure form
a cruel and unusual lotusland
a species of euphoric violence
invincible lack of consequence.

Junkies nod off. In the fortress
of a fix. They drop their fits from
nerveless hands – you can track
the users through the streets. But

heroin has the Mahatma effect.
And those with darkened eyes
the amok-runners with a kris
the beserkers of the Norse

who ritualised bog myrtle for
their trance of fury have their
descendants here – and now
seek to transcend deep shame.

– I Like That Clown

He is as louche as absinthe when the water hits it.
He might like that clown, that clown you painted,

that gapes a toothless pit of a mouth in a black house
because he has eaten all his children. And clowns are

funny. He is an ovum towards which the spermatozoa
swim. The zygote with a single cell is a contract for a

birth, with royalties. A drop of names, a list of shorts,
a line of heads, and in due time, an obit. That glances

o'er a life, a hand that trembled onstage, shook down
the petals of the beautiful mournful autumn roses. He

says a judicious thing, a non-committal – *hm hm hm.*
He sketches an abstract, he proffers a gloss, he sings.

He likes the way the sea looks as black rules silver. Says
– *I like that vivid clown that screams with silent laughter.*

What I Found

Six buttons, by the bus stop, one was tartan
one was cracked, I threw it away, and then

I found a yellow paperclip, slightly splayed.
I saw a hairclip but I didn't want it. Left it.

I found a balcony above the common ruck
a man who shimmered as he spoke like ...

I found a girl clothed in gooseflesh teetering
on Tinakori Road. I found her a taxi, simple.

By lifting one arm. I found a torch and then
a rose garden, and the will to purloin roses.

And I found this.

Absurd Hats 1909

Filmed by James McDonald

Lady Ward (Theresa) was renowned for the size of her hats
her husband's hat is just as ridiculous although vertiginous
hers is an intricacy of folds and tucks – his is a chimney.

Their marital glance, uncertain, as they flicker in the garden
mouthing – *What should I say? Is that machine working?*
but they seem accustomed to hoisting hats out of proportion.

The Threepenny Kowhai Stamp Brooch

If I get lost someone will pick me up and post me.
I am already licked and stamped on my green lapel.

The brooch from Te Papa will see me safely home.
It's 3^D – as in LSD – pounds, shillings and pence.

Let us go out and do the *passegiata* on the waterfront.
If and when I get lost, you can slide me into the red box.

Of course I will be posted back into the past –
back to when kowhai was pronounced kowhai.

The Stamp

for Rita Angus 2008

Tree *1943* brought my letters from home.
Graceful tree, fruitless tree, a framework
with three birds, paused in their passing.

The 45^c stamp that sent my letters Overseas.
To me. For me. Just for me. My stamp. Like
my painting – Central Otago *1953–56/69*. Mine.

Still hanging in the upstairs gallery of my mind.
I can visit it at any time. With grave rapture and
a tender concern and alarm – *What does that cost?*

Then, as if you loved me and longed to meet with me
I slept in The Artist's Studio *circa 1962*. A magnolia tree,
another tree, I took everything I could lay my hands on.

This is the end of it – I said to myself – as I allowed
your house to decay around my head. – *You are gone.*
Silence is gathering and will reclaim what it owns.

Now you unfurl your cigarette and beret above our city,
above your Life & Vision, above your handmaidens,
your gatekeepers, your aficionados, your devotees.

Now I read the book of your life and find – am I yours?
are you mine? – that on the day I was born *12th Oct 1949*
you broke your mind and life to begin again. Frisson!

Not Even Of The Sky

The house is a trap with windows, full of the work
that will never be done. The cobwebs belong to you.
The narrow door is hard to find but you stumble on it.

The time capsule in the roof cavity groans with alarm,
the unworn clothes draped on the foot of the iron bed
simply acquiesce. The heater ticks with an ancient cool.

Downhill, downhill, what is it you are looking for?
As the house forgets you, as you forget the house.
Other houses, neat as safety pins, cute as buttons,

as empty as the beloved whose perfection is served
from afar, by drudgery, by dreaming, are above it all.
They are lonely. Sometimes they tremble, obdurately.

You are scanning the pavement for a useful paper clip.
Or something extraordinary. Something that will keep
you safe forever. The executive wing of democracy,

a man on a horse punching the sky, a rooftop crane
for lifting the city into place, a lion, and a unicorn.
The boys in aprons are smoking in the loading dock.

*

Throngs of young people in black gowns, square caps,
the arcane hoop of rose pink silk hangs down their back,
are talking to each other through their mobile phones

as their parents hammer out snap after snap after snap.
In the city there is LOTTO, there is PROTOPLASM,
there is a face uptilted to the sky, there is a bouquet.

This chapter ends with a golden weed, a dandelion,
the steepest street that ever you saw called Vivian.
Meanwhile SUNDAY HOME DELIVERY at 353.

*

The red circle Liquor-Free Zone (no bottle no glass)
has driven out the recidivist drunks towards the hills
and here they worship the cask on the picnic table

with huddled ceremonies, with the gift of tongues.
The camera wants them, wants their homelessness,
captures a tree, a gnarled old tree, and the traffic.

And turns her fist to take the Tableau Of The Lost,
to take them home with her in a box, but – *Hey!* –
their signalman calls out – *You can't take photos here!*

The camera stutters – *Not even of the sky?* – looses
off a shot not of the sky but of earth and leaf litter.
She folds herself away with a sly wheezing echo.

The figures in the landscape are sentient, possess
antennae, and can speak. Do speak. And command
red circle (no camera) – like in the Sistine Chapel.

*

You can't find where you used to live, several times
– *everything now everything now* – then you find
where you used to live – the pavement is whispering

– *everything now* – the stairs still lead down to the door.
This poem should end with a notorious desk but it ends
with an ironing board crouching alertly at number 14.

Against The Silences To Come

fr david mitchell

She is holding the faded blue chapbook in her hand
                        looking at herself looking at herself
she has carried it across the sea
                        & back again
                                                across the sea
                        & back again
& she didn't know why
                    until now.
                                The return of the ampersand.
Poets used ampersands back then
                                he did
& so did Ron Loewinsohn
                        who wrote AGAINST THE SILENCES TO COME
                        Copyright © 1965 – Four Seasons Foundation
                        Distributed by City Lights Books
                        FOR JOAN

                                        *

There is news of him.
                    There is news to hand.
                                            News has come in.
There is news of the poet who gave her
                        AGAINST THE SILENCES TO COME
in the kitchen of his flat in
                        – as the taxi driver quipped –
                        Sentimental Road.
Where he gave birth to a typewriter
                        while the refrigerator was 'making cold'.
His surname is written
                        on the buffer page
                                        & the ancient price
& below
                        her name.

                                        *

He is moored in a nursing home in Sydney

                        incapable of speech

                            silent

            his hand speaks for him

                on the page

she finds

        she is not sorry for him

                    has no pity

                        she finds

                                in fact

            she has been furious with him

from since then until now

                    since he picked her up & dropped her

                    all in one night.

                            *

He is sitting in the Babel Cafe

                    waiting for his wife & daughter

to dock tomorrow

        – 'on the waterfront' –

                he has bought a painting

                for his daughter's room

                it's mostly pink.

Now

    she supposes

            that he was drunk.

                        That habitual drunkenness

                    that comes across like charm

                        up to a certain point.

Tomorrow doesn't count.

                From tomorrow he would not …

                    but tonight

                once more for luck.

She supposes that she supposed

that she was safe because

– *'I write poetry too.'*

*

& yet the gift.

I find on the last page of his famous book

'silences

to

come?'

I find a grief

a small grief

a small grief like a sharp stone in my smart shoe

fr him.

Everything Is For A Very Short Time

The Penguin Book of New Zealand Verse
Edited by Ian Wedde and Harvey McQueen
1985

There is no question of regret – I write hastily, in the shadow of my hand –
we left off loving – I'm not good I'm not peaceful I'm not wise – collapsing
out of Heaven – good intentions – other disappointments – such an ecstasy
of bewildered weeping – we had to be terrible news – in these terrible times.
Nothing innocent lasts long – the tragic scent of violets – in a broken vase –
her face moves like the face of a thief at the window – her face unclenches
like a fist – yes, the cold has come again – with a diffident explanation.
Theology and a patchwork absolute – the bare longing of the imagination –
treacherous as an avalanche poised above – and the white snake dead too –
the translucent hyperboles of art – saying Bravo Bravo to the Invisible –
eyes lit up by eager, cruel fires – as the taniwha is raised up from its den –
prodded into stuttering rage – his gnarled his dazzling his stubborn heart –
where the visions start – among immortal things – and all this in fidelity
to death – the iron bells toll – my story comes to its end. But picture me.

*[Cento from – Mary Ursula Bethell, Michael Harlow, Meg Campbell, Brian Turner,
Ian Wedde, Bill Manhire, Hilaire Kirkland, Allen Curnow, Tuini Ngāwai (Translation
by Kumeroa Ngoingoi Pēwhairangi), Tony Beyer, A.R.D. Fairburn, Christina Beer,
Elizabeth Nannestad, Sam Hunt, K.O. Arvidson, Denis Glover, Heather McPherson,
Murray Edmond, Alistair Campbell, Fleur Adcock, C.K. Stead, Janet Frame, Keith
Sinclair, Waikato (Translation by Margaret Orbell), M.K. Joseph, Kevin Ireland,
Charles Brasch, Vincent O'Sullivan, James K. Baxter, David Mitchell, Keri Hulme.]*

A Man, Somewhere In History, Dying

Somebody somehow had a cache of film and a recording device.

To shoot the man sinking into the snow drift and looking up
in some Russian city under siege all those black and white
years ago.

And the light went out of his eyes, now we watch him die
and we can watch him die tomorrow, if we want to, and
the day after.

He gives his death, of hunger and cold and despair, to us.

Epicentre

I woke up dazed
some taniwha had risen
underneath my bed
straight up from

the centre of the earth
and humped like
a green horse
first time under the saddle.

Then the noise
a peremptory growl
travelling away from me
as swiftly as a train.

How unusual and strange.
I couldn't write a poem
for every earthquake
I have lived through

they all have their little quirks
but every other one had rumbled
towards me, done its worst
shivered, rippled, shook

then galloped away.
The house and I settled
down, drew our breath
and the earth turned.

Invitation To A Function

Dressed within discrete limits
neither chic nor down-at-heel
we treat the live saxophonist
as if he isn't there.

The marquee on the Square
decked with dry arrangements
is the venue for this Farewell
in Graduation Week.

One of the suits takes the stage
tells the usual story of a life
with wry asides that a stranger
can't understand.

But there is an undercurrent
that shivers through the tent
like a cold breeze blowing in
that portends a change.

The whisper is that he was shafted
he looked away, his job was gone
so willy-nilly he retires, sidelined
from this game.

He is handed an empty envelope,
a hideous metaphor we ignore,
because the tickets for the rugby
aren't available yet.

So we celebrate his working life
a message in the Memory Box
that is the way they do it here.
I am a stranger, I leave town.

Palmy

Some injudicious thoughts about this city. Nothing else can be written.
I perch in my flat on top of the Square at that dullest hour before dawn,
wreathed in Happy by Clinique For Men from Farmers in the Plaza.
I lurk in the mirrored department of luxury and when the girls go off
to mend their hair and drink tea I spray at random. I love perfume
but don't want to smell the same night after night as the bed warms.
The gay club across the yard has spilled the revellers out into the street.
Their music woke me up, the old tunes I remember like 'Dancing Queen.'
I've had the best time ever! – as the barman dumps bottles in the skip.
So now it is just me and the night, and you, and soon the big old moon
riding the clouds of gathering light behind the glass in my high window.
This used to be all forest, not so long ago, and I could tell by the sorrow
that haunts the wide, flat roads, that seeps out of the sense of openness,
something is missing, something is wrenched askew, as the river runs.
The wind blows through, in rolling gusts, baffled, and almost angry.
The wind is searching for the Papaioea Forest. How beautiful it was.
Tonight, behind the necklace of glittering lights below, is the darkness
which is the hills. Upon them, when it is light, like many crucifixions,
the wind farm. Then the long, ungainly arms swoop and seem to bless.
I will admit, to you, that I have found Palmerston North disconcerting.
It is the only word which fits, and I have rummaged the *Thesaurus*.
The thing that throws me most onto the wrong foot and unnerves me
is that I think the father of my first grandchild must be Rangitāne.
He is adopted, doesn't know his kin, nobody we know looks like him.
But here I see his way of walking up ahead of me in Rangitikei Street,
and then the gesture of his hand at the wheel of a car as I cross now,
or he is stooping in a shop door, fitting tiles. His very particular smile.
He has cousins living here. But the link is broken, everything is lost.
We don't know them and they don't know us. There's no way back.
It's a secret we can't unravel. And soon I will be gone. Meanwhile
the wind searches out the last of the autumn roses and shakes them.

Keeble's Bush

Scientific Reserve And Forest Restoration Project

We are stood on the hill looking down upon the finest remnant
of indigenous lowland forest (podocarp-broadleaf) in the district.
It is under attack from old man's beard, and blackberry etcetera,
invasive wandering willy, possums, stoats, rats, mice and from us.
>   The botanist in muddy boots had great hopes of
>   avian flu but it came to nothing this time round.
> The only northern rata has just died.
> Nobody knows how the bush unzips.
> There is no reason for a tree to die.
> But they do die. Nobody knows why.
>   The botanist in muddy boots asserts that if humanity
>   was extinct this land would be claimed by wilding pine.

We step in under cover through the shelter belt with grasses underfoot
passing onto the original bush duff that holds the secret we can't crack.
> Nobody knows how to put it all back together again.
> We don't know, can't know, every element it contains.
> And on my muddy boots might be the spore that splits
> the crystal of this ecosystem apart. It is somehow all my fault.
>   The botanist in muddy boots strokes a kawakawa
>   for cryptic caterpillars on the heart-shaped leaves.

This patch survives because of the useful spring, there is always water
flowing down the hill. When the stream that enters from above is dry,
when it fails, still the water flows although the spring cannot be found.
There is an ungraspable metaphor, a sunlit hymn in a long ago church.
>   The botanist in muddy boots speaks of naive birds
>   as the fantail perks and flutes about our progress.

The Topography Of Wellington

There is a darkness here: and also an itinerant rainbow
strolling like a twister with one lazy finger dipped in water.
There is a harbour: because of the rainbow there may be
a glory, like a saint's halo, which is an optical effect. Glory.

There are six kererū in Orangi-Kaupapa Rd feeding on miro:
or pūriru, tawa, taraire. These birds are almost too indolent
to fly, the telephone wires zig-zag under their exiguous feet.
As they pause – in their top heavy survey of topography, let

us consider our understanding of living above. Above contains
below. Look up to the hills and sky, look down the way a river
runs. You are having it both ways now. The sun seeks you out.
In the deep of night before dawn the wind and the rain blow in.

Look down into this glittering city, high on your slippery hill and
shrug. Would they have called it View Rd if it didn't have a view?

Gleaners

I find buttons on the street
she finds playing cards
if she won't pick one up
the wind blows it to
the next bus stop.
Soon she will have a full pack.
I have a crick in my neck
from looking down for
the next self-shank or flat.
I think of people
with their clothes agape.

Street View

I install Google Earth
– it takes some time –
behold! the Planet.
Where I live.
I touch the cursor
swim downwards
– or perhaps I fall –
towards Australia
and the very house
the husband bought
with my blessing
on a no fault bonus.
Looks quite leafy
huddled in trees
close to the shops
and the station.
But strangely murky
as I juggle to view it
from street level
– that's a new function –
due out soon. People
with cameras are even
now! driving your street
filming your letterbox.
It's not real time
– the mistake I made –
they are shooting us from
the past into the future.

In Australia

The First Drummer Boy Of Xmas

Yesterday I was at the Mall and I heard
my first rendition of Little Drummer Boy.

Dear Lawd above – I said to myself –
Xmas is hard upon us. For our sins.

It is time to head down the back paddock
with the chain saw and harvest a likely tree.

But alas, we have moved away from the place
that has feral and unwanted pine trees aplenty

which as far as I can see are basically weeds
although the local squatter made good money

selling them up in the Big Smoke come December.
What useless things they are. You can't eat them,

they don't burn well, they flare up and spit resin,
they poison the ground around them, nothing grows.

Except toadstools. Plump and gaudy like Xmas bells.
Deck them for their brief season, then chuck them.

At our new house I found the corpse of Xmas past
under the lemon tree. I put it on the burning pile.

Roll on autumn. Pa rum pa pa rum.

Peaches

Now you are making me laugh and remember.
We had a peach tree next to our septic tank.
Over the years the tree had dug its roots
well and truly right into the good muck.

The taste of those peaches! Hot and sweet!
Many in the village would come and beg
for a bucket of the good peaches, the peaches
shaped like buttocks, with a pink flush.

I would try to (tastefully) tell them exactly why
the flavour was so excellent – *You are eating us.
Our ordure, our guano.* But it never put them off.
It was a clingstone peach with a golden flesh.

The rosellas and the bowerbirds would get drunk
and disorderly on the ripe fruit up in the boughs.
I would climb – go eyeball to eyeball with them –
reach out a hand and slap them out of the tree.

Then the Council told us to get a new system
and damn! Those peaches weren't as golden.

The Sea Is Salt, And So Are Tears

The world has become very different.
Just give me a moment.
Since they told me my child was missing
and I knew she had died.

This is my last duty as a father
to seek her body out
and bring her home
and bury her.

But suddenly and slowly and quickly
the world has become different
without her.
I need a moment.

Let me stare at this difference
and try to understand it.
There is before – and there is now.
And there will have to be weeping.

The Death Of Your Brother

I had met him just the once,
he was like you, a likeable chap.
He was like you to look at.

He gave me the cold shoulder.
I could go to hell in my own way
and he wouldn't put a finger out.

But friends will do that for friends
when the wife is being difficult.
He and my husband went way back.

And then he fell off a mountain.
We got the call in our shabby flat.
The husband gasped – I held him up.

Now I don't like snow – it's horrid and cold –
but I was dreaming snow during the darkness
reaching out for a handful of snow.

Then I was falling down down and down
– smack into a drift. Thinking wildly –
That was lucky, I could have killed myself.

I was babbling – *It didn't hurt* – as my friends
came slogging kneedeep to help me out.
It didn't hurt at all. How strange is that!

But they wouldn't talk to me, looking past me,
their faces sad and silent. I was beside myself.
And then it was the opposite of falling.

Listening To 774 ABC Melbourne

Black Saturday February 7th 2009

Kylie rang and asked –
Should I evacuate?
Where should I go?

And he said – *Kylie,*
your fire plan should be in place.
Like the headmaster of the world.

I glanced at the nervous husband sitting
at the foot of the table opposite from me

and I said – *If I was Kylie I would sue him*
for being an utter prick when I needed him.

Bad Day

Black Saturday February 7th 2009

Oh fuck it was a bad day.
It was so bad.
I knew it couldn't end well.
I could smell it wouldn't end well.

I sat up to midnight with 774 radio
listening to what was going down.
I knew most of it wouldn't be on air
and most of it wasn't as it turned out.

It was so bad. It was so bad.
I watched the shopping channel
and did my ironing
to be useful –

one likes to be useful
in the middle of a catastrophe.
As dawn broke I risked cracking
the early morning news.

I shouted to the sleeping husband
– *Marysville has gone!*
As I had ironed – carefully –
his shirts and my blouses

and all of the tea towels
– because I am obsessive –
people had been looking
into the black heart of fire.

What To Pack

Well, first, obviously, you pack your Life. So in it goes.
Funny how you discover it is the one thing you really want.
Or perhaps you could tuck it under one arm as you sprint
away from the firefront or dive headfirst into the bunker.

Then those you love. Maybe you are the kind of people
who pack them first but alas I have found out I am not.
I'm a Me First sort of girl. It's not pretty but it's true.
So those that I love, you know who you are,
into the suitcase which is all that I can carry.

And if I can carry just a little more, a few that are running
down the road screaming. If I can I'll scoop them up. I'm sorry,
there's only room for a few. And the neighbour's ginger cat.

Now we have gone beyond necessity into what we want to still possess
once it is all over. The husband and I had deep and meaningfuls in passing
about his baby photo, in a hand-smocked blouson affair, and my Parker pen.

I had given all my back-up discs in a vast Tupperware container to my daughter.
All the grand projects that are never going to be written but that I can't let go of.
So I was cool about that. All my grand projects. Safe.

But I don't want to appear on Channel 10 saying – *What I stand up in.*
So often it is shorts and the shoe kind of thongs. I packed my good underwear.
I had made a score at a sale – wonderful underwear – pink and ivory and black.
Me tucked away all lovely in labels – with underwires. I packed all that.

And the photo of the children, all grave with sullen lower lips,
the gorgeous pale blue raincoat from Hong Kong,
the knitting with the German needles for the long hours in the shelter,
a lip salve and my happy pills and a hairbrush and my denture glue,
and I ought to add a book that I really want to read.

At last I get a chance at Proust.

And then it is all over and you unpack. Maybe you smile at one strange artefact.
A rusty bottletop. A 30th birthday present from a cat. Don't ask. Or something
even stranger and why you wanted it you forget.

Local Knowledge

Our fire siren can sound at any time and it gets all the dogs in the village barking.
If you can hear the siren down in Upper Ferntree Gully as well then it may be serious.
The stretch of Burwood Highway down out of the Yarra Ranges is called the Mad Mile.
In 1916 my village wanted a street lamp removed because it was 'Made in Germany'.
A man with one arm can often be found drinking in the beer garden of The Bell Tavern.
There is no post office in Tecoma. We have a new postmaster (and his wife) in Upwey.
Upwey is named after a village in Dorset in the Wey Valley near the source of the Wey.
Thomas Hardy used it in 'The Trumpet Major' and 'At The Railway Station, Upway.'
There are some things I can't tell you because I live here. They are my neighbours.
I just won't go to that restaurant again. Although it is usually busy as I walk home.
Once a year buckets of cheap daffodils appear for sale outside places of business.
We have daffodil farms close by, grown for their bulbs, the flowers are surplus.
I arrived in this village as the buckets of rare blooms appeared on the pavement.
They are my marker, one year since I arrived in Upwey. Then two years, and so on.
Our roundabout is a death trap. And the careless way cars swoop down Morris Road.
I saw a car full of young lads nearly lose it as I was waiting for the bus to Oakleigh.
They were drifting, about to roll, but somehow kept going and shot off unrepentent.
Twice in our first week the Give Way sign was smashed flat. The second time it broke.
My husband saw an older chap come in over the bridge going the wrong way around.
I have seen a cop car lurking up by the Fire Station. Poised to intercept offenders.
But enough of traffic. Enough of the boy racers up on the hill roads of a Saturday night.
The kids in our village smashed the myki machine on the station. It has been replaced.
Every week, fresh graffiti. The man in the overalls with the paint pot keeps on painting.
The kids smash the shop windows too. Why? We should sit them down and ask them.
The bus trip up to Mt Dandenong is a cheap thrill. You look down and see Melbourne.
But of course, we are Melbourne too. Look on any map. The hills are part of the city.
Our garden is vertiginous. We can't do backyard cricket, we go in for bungy jumping.
The Mountain Ash forest, a parade of lofty, beautiful sisters, is an abiding presence.
As the fire season approaches, our siren can go off at any time and all the dogs will bark.

Lost Property

Somewhere in the city
I lost the knitting
the sentimental wool
I had unpicked to reknit.

The colour scheme was alarming
but that was what my mother chose
when she was still capable of crochet
so I held my peace and flew her colours.

I had been warned of an imminent loss
the knowledge of loss had thrummed by
so I kept checking I had everything
one hand delving in my shoulderbag.

And more than the knitting is the pillowcase
made by my husband's mother, now deceased,
she had run it up from a summery cotton frock
with two ties at the top to keep the knitting safe.

My hands know the scarf in progress intimately
I was working away at the royal blue stripe
plain and plain and plain and plain again and turn
the yarn between my fingers running like smoke.

As I rose to leave my train at Upwey Station
a thud of portent hit me – something missing –
my soft bundle pierced by two sharp needles.
And my hands, now, disconsolate as ghosts.

How To Cast Off

I poised the needles to do the final thing
you can do for a shawl (before the fringe)
and forgot, forgot how to cast off.

My hands blanked out how to do it and
I have done it a hundred hundred times
I got a fright.

I walked around the house for a bit
but it didn't come back. I sat.
Learning how not to know something.

I still knew what a selvedge looks like.
And I still knew wool.
I put two and two together.

And worked it out.
Yes, it was late. I was tired. But
casting off had slipped away from me.

The Raspberry-Coloured Hand-Knitted Cardigan

For a quick ecstatic moment I think – *Herdwick double knit!*
Just what I need to unravel and reknit for the poet's jumper.

And then my fingers know it for a triple and it is not Herdwick.
But still. I rethink my project, my brain goes click click click.

It is knit deliciously wrong side out with a cool curving basque.
The buttons are a wry comment on the high concept of 'cardigan'.

It's a piece of work. But it is so small, who could it possibly fit?
Not her it was knitted for, over slow ticking hours, it is pristine.

Fallen fresh from the needles of a woman who can really knit.
It would be a sin to undo her gift. It would be mortally wrong.

Wool remembers what it was and would resist such declension.
Such consummate sewing up of it, such a smooth, even tension.

If it is still hanging on the rack on Tuesday when I go back
I will buy it for eight bucks, salvage the buttons, and unpick.

The Crowded Train

I am looking down
at a blind man's legs
and his white stick.

Then I see a wedding ring
on an old man's hand
close up.

The girl next to me
is a voice
and the smell of wet.

She was stuck at Richmond
I was caught at Laburnum
the sky spoke *in extremis.*

The rain was horizontal
the wind blew us together
onto this very late train.

I am the brim of my hat
perhaps, or a glance
from under it.

Alamein

At Camberwell she chants – *Change here for the Alamein line.*
So I did because my uncle used to say that word in a certain way.

Riversdale Willison Hartwell Burwood Ashbuston Alamein.
I was the only person who got off here. And nobody got on.

A bemused and indolent suburb, stunned by peace.
A slow car bumbling through the shadows of trees.

A shop with a tiny woman behind the tower of tic-tacs
and the deep throb of the drinks fridge by the sticky door.

I looked around for a war memorial but I could find none.
Just an insignificant station like the original El Alamein.

The sunshine and the lazy trees and the somnolent ease
are a true memorial for my uncle and the men like him.

Imagining Jane

Jane Austen would have given her high buttoned boots
thrown in the corset and the gentility imperative
to have had as much sex as she wanted with Mr Darcy
with a bit of Wickham on the side, if she was in the mood.
When she found out he was a prick she could have dumped him.

Then, enough of this scraping by on £50 a year,
she could have got a job and earned her own living.
She could have been a copywriter, she had a fair idea
what women wanted, or thrown her cap over the windmill,
learned how to fly a plane. Her restless hands on the joystick.

She could have stood on the railway platform and screamed
– *I just want to go out and get fucking shitfaced and get fucked.*
Or she could have been waiting for the train in a well-cut suit,
jotting down local mores and tricks of speech in a discreet notebook.
She could have been a novelist, that would have been right up her street.

She might have tasted heroin, she might have enjoyed the cafe society.
She might have liked getting legless at some rough pub, in the spirit of research.
She might have travelled with a lightweight suitcase, which she carried herself,
packed with mix 'n' match, quick-dry, non-iron gear, and a bottle of Rinse-Thru.
She might have stayed at home and gorged on TV and microwave meals.

She mightn't have understood that she didn't need a man to take her by the arm.
She might have married, set up house, tried to hire a cook and buy a carriage.
I imagine her with children, she was an excellent aunt, I see her as a mother.
I like to think that all the imminent carnage of our times would not phase her.
Napoleon was hammering on her door and she kept her cool, didn't turn a hair.

She would have been bemused, I know, at modern females wanting to fly back
into the muslin prison, the bonnet and gloves, the petticoat dragging in the mud.
Riding side-saddle, your spine twisted to face front, childbirth with no drugs.
And the disease she died of – *'I must not depend on ever being blooming again'* –
although we can't agree upon what it was, she may have bloomed longer than 41.

Imagining Emily

She is setting a pan of milk on the larder shelf
then, wiping her fingers on her coarse apron,
making the sign – tick a lock – the key in the door.
My work is done so my work can begin.

Her apron swings from the nail on the wall,
the whisk tocks to and fro on the window sill.
Or I could be wrong. I was never there.
Where would the whisk animate itself?

On the draining board? Beside the crock?
I have an empty kitchen. She climbs the stairs.
I can see the door she cracked open to hear
the words spoken at her father's funeral.

She is a freeze-frame of white angles ascending
to where the sleigh bed gallops her away at night
with words like the plumes on horses' heads.
And waiting for her, her imaginary friends.

And here, such silliness, I imagine, amongst others,
the louche ex-drummer from The Three Lost Chords
his face a road map that has been folded up too often.
Here's Em! – he shouts. *Let's jam. Let's rock and roll.*

Some of her familiars have lived in books, and some
are hardly human, Chanticleer imprints his tracks.
I summon a French nun with a vinegar tongue, some,
like me, are a dim presentiment of what will come.

The Dead Woman's Button Box

This is an anecdote, which is a kind of singing, from the Greek, *anekdota* –
unpublished items. These are the hitherto undivulged particulars of her history.

This is a button box, although it is a cake tin, it is a tin in spite of being plastic.
It has an orange and brown floral trim, so it has to be from plump in the fifties.

I take off the lid and release the gamy smell of kitchen grease, wet dog, old age.
I can see straight off that she didn't favour blue but preferred the peach spectrum.

A family member was in the Military, all the embossed buttons with metal shanks.
And they did have a dog at some stage, I find the registration tag, kept as a token.

There was a husband in the picture, with a fly he buttoned up and unbuttoned.
The sombre fixings, the doings and undoings, rattle around at a complete loss.

And the dross, the pins, tacks and washers, a dresser handle, and tiddlywinks.
Which I toss as I sift, the mostly buttons falling like water through my fingers.

I never met her. All I can know of her is what I can infer from this psychometry.
Some buttons are so old and crazed I think she inherited them from her mother.

A nail clipping, just one. The moment when she snipped and it pinged off, gone.
This is a precious relic, containing all her secrets, her lineage and her character.

I sluice and scrub the buttons, set them to dry and winnow in the afternoon sun.
They begin to shine and speak to me, soon I will own them, they will be mine.

Table Of Contents

The anthology of Australian Women's Poetry
fell quickly, according to the Introduction, into
the twelve sections. That you see here. There.
I was reading like a herbivore, eating pages.

Nature and Icons and Pregnancy and Birth.
Infancy, Sons & Daughters, Daily Grind, Loss.
Old Wives' Tales, Mothers & Grandmothers,
The World and This Last Retreat. All neat.

I raised my head from the handsome book
and stared into the big whatwasmissing.
Where were the Fathers & Brothers?
Where were the Husbands & Lovers?

Where were those good looking bastards who
have had their way with me time and again?
Where was the delicious catastrophe of Men?

I Came Home With The Shopping

And I said to him as he opened the front door –
Do you remember what day it is tomorrow?
And he said – *No. What day is it?*

Then I said – *Do you remember who you married?*
Yes – he said. *Yes. I do remember her.*
And then we both said – *How many years is it?*

Should we do something? – he said. *No* – I said.
Let's just do what we always do. I like doing that.

Sunday Afternoon In Kings Park

Africa has come to Kings Park
the families could have walked here
three billion years ago when Ur
was the only continent on earth.

Women with bright cloth
wrapped about their heads
men saunter where they will
kids are rolling down the hill.

A young black man says when asked
– *I am from Tanzania.*
He rhymes Tanzania with Australia.
We are all walking on the English sward.

And upside down as it likes to be
another African cousin, a Boab tree,
trucked in from Warmun in the Kimberley
begins to sprout in the Two Rivers Lookout.

Acknowledgements

'All Together Now: A Digital Bridge for Auckland and Sydney', artsACT,
*Best New Zealand Poems 2009, Blackmail, Bravado, Cordite Poetry Review,
Enamel, Eureka Street, Island, JAAM, Manawatu Standard, New Zealand Books,
Overland, Poetry Ireland Review, Poetry London, Poetry New Zealand, Quadrant,
Reconfigurations, Reflecting On Melbourne, Takahē, The Canberra Times,
The Poetry Kit, Water, Westerly, Writers Connect.*

My sincere thanks for the support of ~
the Liguria Study Centre in Bogliasco, Italy,
the Creative NZ Randell Writers Trust in Wellington, New Zealand,
Community Arts Palmerston North, New Zealand,
and the School of English and Media Studies, Massey University, New Zealand.

Randell Cottage
Writers Trust

Jennifer Compton was born in Wellington in 1949. Between the early 1970s and '80s she worked as a playwright in both Australia and New Zealand, with productions on radio and in theatre in both countries. She has written and had produced or published many stage and radio plays and short stories and essays. Her stage play, *The Big Picture*, which premiered at the Griffin Theatre in Sydney in 1997, was published by Currency Press and also produced in Wellington by Circa and Perth by the Perth Theatre Company. She has won several Australian awards for poetry and has been an invited writer at literary festivals in Australia and internationally.